A DK PUBLISHING BOOK

For Jasia Holdsworth-Lisicki

Written by Mary Atkinson
Art Editor Mandy Earey
Deputy Managing Editor Dawn Sirett
Deputy Managing Art Editor
C. David Gillingwater
US Editor Camela Decaire
Production Josie Alabaster
Picture Research Angela Anderson

First American Edition, 1997
2 4 6 8 10 9 7 5 3 1
Published in the United States by
DK Publishing, Inc., 95 Madison Avenue, New York, New York 10016
Visit us on the World Wide Web at http://www.dk.com

Copyright © 1997 Dorling Kindersley Limited, London

A CIP catalog record for this book is
available from the Library of Congress.

ISBN 0-7894-2057-0

Color reproduction by Chromagraphics, Singapore
Printed and bound in Italy by L.E.G.O.

The publisher would like to thank the following for their kind
permission to reproduce their photographs:

t=top, b=bottom, l=left, r=right, c=center, BC=back cover, FC=front cover

Barzilay PR: (Why does my friend wear ...?)tl; **Chris Fairclough Colour Library:**
endpapers, (Why do some people use wheelchairs?)tr; **Edmund Clark** (Why do some
buildings ...?)tr; **Format Photographers:** Judy Harrison (Why do some people feel
sorry ...?)bl; **Sally and Richard Greenhill:** (Why do some people feel sorry ...?)br;
Guide Dogs for the Blind: Stephen Markeson (Why does Dad ...?)br; **Robert Harding
Picture Library:** (Why does my friend wear ...?)br; **Photofusion:** David Montford
(Why can't my brother ...?)bl; **Tony Stone Images:** FC c, (Why do some people use
wheelchairs?)c, Terry Vine (Why can't my brother ...?)c, Stewart Cohen BC c, (Why
does Dad ...?)c, Don Smetzer (Why does Dad ...?)bl, Will and Deni McIntyre (Why do
some people read ...?)c, Mary Kate Denny (Why do some people read ...?)tr;
Telegraph Colour Library: Robert Clare (Why do some buildings ...?)c, M. Goddard
(Why does my friend wear ...?)c, (Why can't some people with hay fever ...?)c;
Zefa: (Why do some buildings ...?)bl, (Why do some people feel sorry ...?)c.

Additional photography by Andy Crawford, Steve Gorton,
Ray Moller, Susannah Price, Jules Selmes.

Questions

Why do some people use
wheelchairs?

Why can't my brother go
to my school?

Why does Dad wear glasses
when he's reading?

Why do some buildings
have ramps as well as stairs?

Why does my friend
wear a hearing aid?

Why do some people read
with their fingers?

Why can't some people
with hay fever have a dog?

Why do some people feel
sorry for disabled people?

WHY

do some people
use wheelchairs?

Questions children ask
about disabled people

Consultant: Alan Holdsworth, Disability Equality Trainer

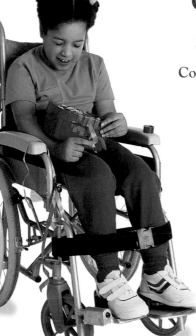

DK PUBLISHING, INC.

Why do some people use

People who don't walk or who find walking tiring or difficult often use a wheelchair to move around. Some people power and steer their chair with their arms, others use a motor.

Why do some people talk with their hands?
Some people who don't hear sounds use hand signals to stand for words. This way of talking is called sign language. Deaf people invented it, and anyone can learn to use it.

wheelchairs?

Why do some people walk with a stick?
Often, people who don't see use a stick to feel what's in front of them. They can quickly tell where there are stairs, walls, or other obstacles by moving the stick around.

Why can't my brother

Not all schools provide the ramps, elevators, and other equipment that make it easy for disabled children to get around. This means some children can't go to the same school as you.

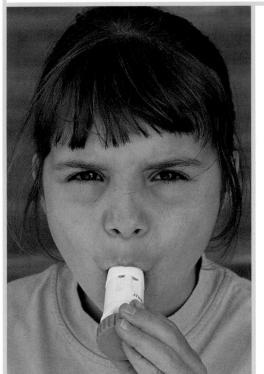

Why do some children take an inhaler to school? Some children with asthma use an inhaler to help them breathe more easily. Playing sports and changes in the weather are some of the things that can make breathing difficult for them, so they take an inhaler to school in case it's needed.

go to my school?

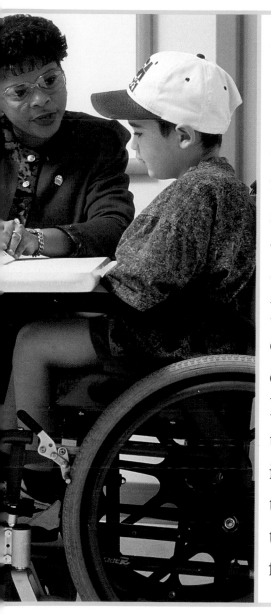

Why do some people take a long time to learn things?
Some people with learning difficulties take longer than most people to learn skills such as speaking and writing. Sometimes they need different kinds of teaching as they learn in different ways. Like anyone, they feel upset if people tease them about the things that they find difficult.

Why does Dad wear glasses

Glasses help many people see. Most people find it harder to see small-sized letters when they grow older, so they wear glasses when they read. Reading glasses are like magnifying glasses – they make the words look bigger.

Why do some older people use walkers? People use walkers if they need extra support when they're moving around. Like walking sticks, walkers help people keep their balance.

when he's reading?

Why shouldn't I pet guide dogs?
Guide dogs are working dogs. They must alert their blind owners whenever they reach a crossing, an obstacle, or the place where they're going. Petting a guide dog could stop it from concentrating. Always ask the owner for permission before you touch or talk to a guide dog.

Why do some buildings have

Why do some parking lots have spaces just for disabled people? Large lots and ones with stairs or narrow spaces can be difficult for disabled people to get around. This is why some parking lots have wide spaces near stores and offices that are for disabled people only.

Stairs are a hard shape to climb for people using wheelchairs. Ramps and elevators, however, allow

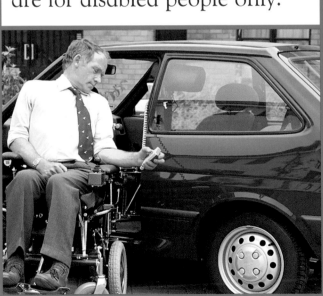

ramps as well as stairs?

most people to get in and out of a building easily without needing to ask anyone for help.

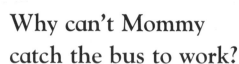

Why can't Mommy catch the bus to work?
The only way to get on most buses is to climb up steps. This means that people who use wheelchairs find it difficult to catch buses. They have to find other ways of traveling until the buses are properly equipped.

Hearing aids make sounds louder. People who don't clearly hear the words other people are saying often wear

Why do some people use machines to talk?
People whose speech isn't easily understood by others sometimes use electronic speaking machines. They push different buttons to make the machines speak different messages. The machines speak the words that have already been recorded onto them.

friend wear a hearing aid?

a hearing aid inside their ear or clipped onto the back of it. The hearing aid helps them hear most sounds.

Why do some people watch your lips when you talk? Some people who don't hear can tell what other people are saying by watching their lips. There's no need to shout at someone who's lip-reading – just don't mumble or put your hands over your mouth.

Many people who don't see learn to read Braille – a type of writing that uses bumps pressed onto paper to stand for letters in the alphabet. They feel the bumps with their fingers to read. People write in Braille using a Braille typewriter. Some books are printed in Braille as well as in ordinary type.

Why do some libraries and bookstores have books on tape?
All sorts of people enjoy listening to novels and interesting facts recorded on tape. They include blind people, car drivers, and children wanting to hear a story.

with their fingers?

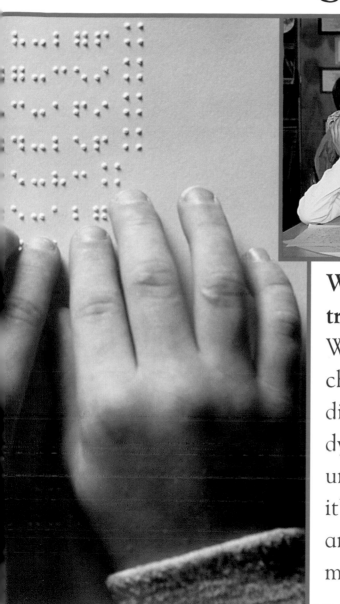

Why do some children have trouble reading and writing?
We all learn at different speeds. Many children find reading and writing difficult at first. Children with dyslexia can find it extra difficult to understand letters and numbers, so it's harder for them. If their parents and teachers realize this, they can make it easier for them to learn.

Pet hair, pollen, dust, and certain foods are all things that can make some people feel ill. They can cause allergic reactions such as hay fever or eczema. The easiest way for people with allergies to stay well is to avoid whatever they're allergic to.

Why shouldn't some people sit too near a TV?
People with epilepsy avoid sitting too close to a television because it can bring on an epileptic fit. They can also have a fit at other times. If someone does have a fit, make sure nothing can hurt or choke them, roll them onto their side, and stay with them if you can.

with hay fever have a dog?

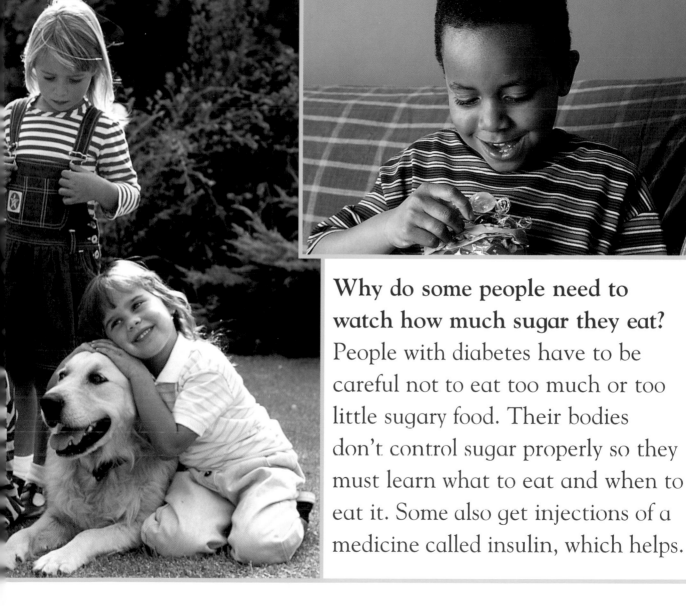

Why do some people need to watch how much sugar they eat? People with diabetes have to be careful not to eat too much or too little sugary food. Their bodies don't control sugar properly so they must learn what to eat and when to eat it. Some also get injections of a medicine called insulin, which helps.

Why do some people feel

Some people think disabled people are unhappy because of their disability. However, most disabled people are busy working and playing – they don't feel unhappy and, like you, don't want other people to feel sorry for them.

Why do some people make fun of disabled people?
When people make fun of other people it's often because they're afraid or unsure of anyone who's different. Yet we are all different, which is good. We have different things to offer and teach each other.

sorry for disabled people?

Why do some people stare at disabled people?

Some people who don't know many disabled people stare whenever they see a disabled person just because they're different. No one likes being stared at, so always think about how a person might feel before you stare.